RIDING

<u>THE</u> SKIES

it's a small world by Speedbird

BRITISH OVERSEAS AIRWAYS CORPORATION IN ASSOCIATION WITH QANTAS EMPIRE AIRWAYS · SOUTH AFRICAN AIRWAYS AND TASMAN EMPIRE AIRWAYS LIMITED

RIDING THE SKIES

CLASSIC POSTERS FROM THE GOLDEN AGE OF FLYING

WITH AN INTRODUCTION BY JAN MORRIS

BLOOMSBURY

Frontispiece:
IT'S A SMALL WORLD BY SPEEDBIRD
Artist: **F.H.K. Henrion**
1947

Bloomsbury Publishing Ltd, 2 Soho Square, London W1V 5DE

This book was first published in Great Britain 1989

Copyright © 1989 Phillips & Company Books, Inc.
Introduction copyright © 1989 Jan Morris

This book was designed and produced by
Phillips & Company Books
4 Doughty Street
London WC1N 2PH

British Library Cataloguing in Publication Data

Riding the skies : classic posters from
the golden age of flying
1. Advertising posters to 1960.
Special subjects. Air travel
I. Morris, Jan
769'.49387742

ISBN 0-7475-0337-0

Designed by Graham Davis Associates, London

Colour separation by Fotographics, Ltd, London/Hong Kong
Typesetting by Florencetype Ltd, Kewstoke, Avon
Printed in Italy

TABLE of CONTENTS

ACKNOWLEDGMENTS

The publishers, and Phillips & Company Books, would like to thank the following people who helped enormously in the preparation of this book:

Sincere thanks, first of all, are due to British Airways—RT. HON. LORD KING OF WARTNABY, Chairman, and JAMES CROALL, Public Affairs Manager—for their kind permission to publish posters from the British Airways Archive.

This book could never have been produced without R.A.R. WILSON, VRD, of the Historical Aviation Service, Ruislip, and Consultant Archivist to British Airways. It was Ron Wilson who first responded with enthusiasm to the idea of this project, and his energetic assistance has never wavered. His generosity has extended not only to his time and archival resources, but also to his wide-ranging knowledge gathered during fifty years in aviation.

WILLIAM McCLAY of Drumahoe Graphics has been unfailingly generous in making available transparencies from his superb series of postcards of this poster collection.

MICHAEL WALTON of the London Transport Museum, Covent Garden, kindly read the manuscript and made many valuable suggestions based on his extensive knowledge of period commercial art.

BRYAN BRONSON produced outstanding special photography with much care and resourcefulness.

STEPHEN F. BREIMER gave wise advice and encouragement, as always.

Exhaustive efforts have been made to identify and contact all the artists whose work has been included in this book, or their heirs. Phillips & Company Books would be extremely grateful for information leading to artists whom we have not been able to find, so that any omissions can be corrected in future editions. To those artists whose work appears, our renewed appreciation.

Many thanks also go to:

IAN BARTLETT

EDWARD BISHOP, RBA

YVONNE BONHAM (Guild of Aviation Artists)

ROSE MARY BRAITHWAITE

PENNY COOPER (Imago Publishing)

JEROME GOLD

RICHARD HAYES (Imago Publishing)

MALCOLM HOARE

NAOMI HOFFMAN

ANNE HUNTER (Imago Publishing)

MATHIAS JABOT

NICHOLAS JELLICOE

PATRICIA JELLICOE

CONSTANCE KEENE

WILLIAM KOSMAS

LYNN MacRITCHIE

DAVID F. PHILLIPS

GORDON PHILLIPS (History of Advertising Trust)

THOMAS PONSONBY

ERIK PORDES (Imago Publishing)

KATE RADFORD (Chartered Society of Designers)

AUBREY RIX

ROY RUBINSTEIN

KEVIN RYAN

RICHARD SACHS

JOYCE SAUNDERS (Imago Publishing)

W. IAN SCOTT-HILL, OBE

JOHN STROUD

EDMUND SWINGLEHURST

PAMELA TODD

CLIVE UPTTON

KELLEY JEANE YOUNGER

Proofreaders: ELIZABETH LONGLEY

ANNA POWELL

MARY SCOTT

INTRODUCTION

BY JAN MORRIS

When the Victorians spoke of trade following the flag, they had in mind an ensign carried at the prow of a gunboat, on a staff above bayonets, or magnificent over the mud hut of a district commissioner in the bush. Nowadays, to most of us, a flag-carrier is a national airline, the most universally known, most easily recognisable instrument of nationality; and among all the airlines of the world, none has been more frank about its loyalties than the distinctly emblematic organisation we know as British Airways.

It was always so. The British built their imperial and commercial power upon their mastery of the means of transport, and when the routes of the air came to rival the routes of the sea, they transferred to their airliners the pride, the pageantry, some of the technique and much of the mystique that they had famously applied to their passenger ships. Other countries might have more enterprising airlines and faster aircraft, but nobody took to the air with more style than the British.

It is above all that style that this book celebrates, through the much-admired series of posters by which the British national airline and its related companies in the Commonwealth, with a characteristic blend of swagger and humour, advertised their services in the Thirties, Forties and Fifties. In later decades the manners of British airlines were to become less distinctive; but in those last fading years of Empire they were unique. I am old enough to remember them—old enough to have taxied to the tarmac in a British airliner from whose cockpit roof there fluttered a ceremonious Civil Air Ensign (hastily pulled down by the co-pilot before take-off), and to have spent a night at the fortified guest-house that Imperial Airways established, for the convenience and protection of its passengers, in the middle of the Iraqi desert. Looking at these bright brilliant posters is like a transference to the past, when it was the coughing of motors, not the whistle of jets, that gave warning of departure, and when, straining to peer out of the cabin window from the half-crippling sitting position (with no wheel under the nose, airplanes sloped violently backwards), you might see lined up below in stiff parade the unmistakably British ground staff saluting you farewell.

Today British Airways, the flag-carrier, is one gigantic and monolithic institution, but its pedigree is mixed. At least thirty airlines have been absorbed down the years into its stream, including the Blackpool and West Coast Air Services, the Daimler Airway, British Air Marine Navigation Company, another British Airways altogether, and the unpromisingly named Spartan Airways (which flew only from London to Cowes). In 1924 it was incarnated as Imperial Airways; the name was changed to British Overseas Airways Corporation in 1939. After World War II it was split for almost thirty years into British Overseas Airways and British European Airways; only in 1974, with a monumental heave of logos, colourings, letterings and arrangements, did it emerge at last as the definitive British Airways.

If this sounds a muddled and tentative progress, it is because Britain itself was moving through these decades uncertainly. Except during the heroic period of world war, the nation was seldom sure of itself. Even in the Thirties the Empire was beginning to fail, and the intense patriotism of Imperial Airways (which would fly no aircraft but British, and would probably have preferred to ignore the existence of Europe) seems in retrospect more endearing than formidable. By the Forties, when I first flew with BOAC, a perceptible air of apology lay behind the stiff upper lip; everyone knew by then that the American airlines, in particular, were far larger, more modern and better equipped. It was really not until the Seventies by which time Britain was finding its new status as a middle-rank European power, that the British flag-carrier acquired a truly professional, contemporary assurance.

All this one may read between the colourful lines of these posters. Proud indeed look the great biplanes and flying boats of Imperial Airways ("*Every* Imperial Air Liner has 4 Engines for Security"), gliding over the Ganges or towering hospitably above their boarding passengers at Croydon Aerodrome. Their ship-like air is deliberate. They are dubbed RMA, Royal Mail Aircraft, as the imperial steamships were dubbed RMS, and they travel along all-red routes of Empire like the shipping lines before them. They are living so to speak on the Empire's more confident past. The airlines of Australia, New Zealand and South Africa flew "in association" with them, as the far-flung possessions existed in association with the mother country; and when Fougasse, in a celebrated poster of 1936, has an Imperial Airways steward confidently trotting above the clouds on his own wings, carrying a meal-tray, it is as if to show that in the skies, as on the sea and land, the Empire still maintains its own imperturbable order.

By the Forties and Fifties, though, the emphasis of publicity was less on grandeur, more on exoticism—less on the Britishness of travel, more on the foreignness of destination. By then the routes of Empire were no longer pre-eminent, the imperial swagger was out of fashion, and the old associates of Empire and Commonwealth were fast becoming rivals. More people were flying for pleasure, far fewer to rule the world. We see the shift of history in these posters.

The long haul was always the British speciality. The all-red routes were the longest in the world, and longest of all was Imperial Airways' flagship service from London to Sydney, maintained in conjunction with Qantas Empire Airways. Ten and a half days to Australia, boasts a poster of 1935, and on it the de Havilland 86 biplane RMA *Canberra* is to be seen airily circling, light and steady on its four engines, somewhere over the Equator. The truth was less effortless.

Even by the late Thirties, when the eastern routes had got well into their stride with the fine Empire class flying boats (twenty-eight of which Imperial Airways bravely bought direct from the drawing-board), the journey was extremely demanding. One left Southampton at 5.15 on a Thursday morning, say, and reached Sydney twenty-nine stops later on the Saturday week. Because there was no night flying, one spent nights on the ground at Athens, Basra, Karachi, Calcutta, Bangkok, Singapore, Surabaya, Darwin and Townsville. On the South African routes the experience could be still more exhausting because, as the 1938 time-table said, calls could be made at Mirabella, Kareima, Kosti, Butiaba, Quelimane and Inhambane "if inducement offers and circumstances permit". It was no joke making such a journey. The aircraft engines were terribly noisy. The cabins were unpressurised. All too often take-offs were hideously early in the morning, and though the overnight hotels included Raffles in Singapore and the Grand in Khartoum, they also included less sybaritic establishments, such as the rest-house at Lombok Island in the Dutch East Indies, where passengers might be required to share beds.

But for all these and other disadvantages the British tried to compensate with an old-school diligence of service. They strove not so much for speed and frequency, like the Americans, but for gentlemanly arrangement; it was customary during the Twenties and Thirties, if a British aircraft was in the air on Armistice Day, for passengers to rise to their feet to observe the national two-minute silence. In the United States flying was becoming a commonplace, but for the British it was sufficiently rare in the Thirties, and sufficiently expensive too, to make every passenger an important person, like someone in a Cunarder's first-class stateroom. The attitude died hard, and it is not so long ago that British airliner captains used to stroll among their passengers from time to time, asking them in a lordly way if everything was all right; when I once had the temerity to ask a captain if he was sure they had enough fuel for the non-stop flight from San Francisco to London, he replied reassuringly, "Oh dear me yes, rest assured, we're terrible cowards up front."

In the days of Imperial Airways, captains used actually to come aft to take luncheon with their passengers, while stewards in white starched jackets served meals freshly cooked on board. A poster from the Thirties perfectly sums up this ambience: a passenger sits, with his feet up, in a deep armchair which is supported only by clouds; debonairly holding a cigarette in his hand, he seems to be waiting for Jeeves himself to come oozing in with the brandy.

I cannot say my own first flight with British Overseas Airways was so suave, and I am not surprised that no poster immortalises it. It was soon after the war. I was weighed in, along with my luggage, at the ramble of tents and huts that constituted in those days the passenger terminal of Heathrow, and lumbered off to Egypt in a converted RAF transport plane called the Avro York. As I examined my oxygen mask and sniffed the greyish cardboard box that contained my lunch, I thought it was probably very like setting off on a mission to Berlin.

Those, however, were makeshift times, when the airline, having lost almost all its pre-war airplanes, awaited their post-war replacements. In fact the British airlines had established a particular reputation for the comfort of their aircraft. They were seldom fastest: if the winds were against them the Handley Page 42 biplanes on the pre-war Paris routes were slower than trains. They were seldom the most up-to-date, either: the Americans were flying their DC-3s, still in service to this very day, at a time when the average British airliner looked like something out of World War I. Just as the Royal Navy, however, preferred warships that looked beautiful, so the British airlines liked to emphasise that their aircraft had urbanity.

It shows very well in these pictures. The Silver Wing service to Paris may indeed have been slow, but the passengers boarding at Croydon in the 1938 poster look well aware that it was claimed to be the most luxurious air service in the whole world—with walnut-panelled cabins, lace-edged curtains, chintz-covered armchairs, sterling silver cutlery, and on the table before each seat a silver vase of fresh flowers. The Empire flying boat *Canopus* looks all agleam, all ample hospitality, as its guests are greeted at the quayside door: there was a promenade deck on those boats, along which passengers might saunter looking out of big porthole windows, a smoking cabin and a little wine cellar; and a typical dinner in the Thirties included pâté de fois gras, roast chicken, ox tongue, York ham, salads, peach Melba, figs, three kinds of cheese, desserts and crystallised fruit.

I experienced what I believe to have been almost the end of this class-conscious exhibition, which essentially aimed at luxury for the rich few rather than convenience for the poorer many. The four-engined Hermes aircraft, which entered BOAC's African service in 1950, seems to me in memory to have been the most comfortable aircraft I ever flew in, and while I dare say this is partly the blur of nostalgia, it may possibly be true: the Hermes, which was technically out of date even before its maiden flight, and which lasted only three years with the airline, was built by Handley Page, the builders of those sybaritic biplanes of the Silver Wing, and really did honour the plush, squashy, club-like armchair heritage of Imperial Airways.

It was the last, I think. After it—modernity. The celebrated Speedbird logo of Imperial Airways, which was designed by the artist Theyre Lee-Elliott in 1932 and embellished British aircraft until 1984, really came into its own after World War II. It was an image of clear-cut power and speed, and in the posters of the later Forties and Fifties the emphasis was not on getting there comfortably, but on being there soon. No longer did the leviathans cast their shadows upon the expanse of Empire. The day of mass air travel was arriving, and in these advertisements the aircraft were generally incidental to scenes of skyscrapers or lagoon, wild life or carnival; sometimes indeed they did not show at all, or were only symbolized.

Gone, all gone, were the Jeeves, the two-minute silence and luncheon at the captain's table. When I first stepped aboard one of BOAC's bulbous double-decker Boeing Stratocruisers, in the early Fifties, it was certainly not Britishness of atmosphere that struck me, but astonishing transatlantic technology; and that glorious aircraft the Lockheed Constellation, for my money the most beautiful of them all with its humped back and three tailfins, projected no suggestion of Empire even with a Union Jack on its tail. As it stood sprung and curved like a cheetah on the tarmac, it always seemed to me an image of the times themselves.

For by then the British flag-carrier had perforce abandoned its all-British policies, just as the New York route had replaced those to India, South Africa and Australia as the airline's flagship service. Echoes of old preoccupations sounded now and then—gleaming stands the Rolls-Royce car, in a poster of the Fifties, beneath the Rolls-Royce turbo-props of a BEA Vickers Viscount. Later, in the Sixties, BOAC's Vickers VC-10 was optimistically presented as a new British aircraft to beat the world. The last great splurge of whole-hog patriotism, however, came with the introduction in 1952 of the de Havilland Comet 1, the first jet airliner. I flew to India on it the following year, and though as a matter of fact we still spent a night in a dingy guest-house at Karachi, and though my own seat, at the back of the aircraft, proved to be unreclinable—very nearly annulling for me the advantages of jet travel—still I remember to this day with what pride I looked back at it, shimmering in the heat, as I walked towards the Delhi terminal—the very latest, the very best, and British all through.

The Comet was withdrawn from service in 1954, after the shattering loss of two aircraft as a result of metal fatigue. Perhaps its tragic failure really was the end of the Imperial Airways tradition, and properly so. The jet age, first revealed to us by the Comet, proved to be an altogether fresh start for air travel when it reappeared to stay in 1958. The golden age of the airlines is probably now. A two-day Boeing 747 to Australia is really much more comfortable, and perhaps more exciting too, than a ten-day flying boat; an Airbus is infinitely less exhausting than one of those lovely Constellations; better a midnight movie than sharing a bed on Lombok Island. Time, like distance, lends enchantment, and when we remember the charm and stately service of Imperial Airways we tend to forget the inconveniences and the hazards that were no less a part of those journeys (nearly a quarter of those Empire flying boats crashed).

But style, yes: for better or for worse, as these posters confirm, the British flag-carriers have always had that, and to this day there is no practitioner more stylish than the British Airways captain at his best. Come Silver Wing come Concorde, he is to the manner born. Sometimes, if he is of the brass-bound, moustachioed, ramrod kind, to be seen marching in an authoritative way across the airline terminal with his crew dutiful in his wake, he could still be the commander of RMA *Canopus*, going ashore for the night's break at Raffles, and occasionally his announcements from the flight deck still have the authentic ring of mingled swank and self-amusement. "I am glad to be able to tell you," I heard one such traditionalist announce recently, "that we shall be landing at JFK ten minutes earlier than scheduled. This is of course entirely due"—dry, well-timed, Imperial Airways pause—"to our incomparable technical brilliance."

T<u>HE</u> POSTERS

<u>THE</u> THIRTIES

BRITISH AIRWAYS

Artist unknown

circa 1936

The British Airways advertised in this lyrical
poster from the mid-Thirties was a precursor of
today's British Airways — the result of a merger,
in 1935, of three small airlines on short-haul
European routes. Four years later British Airways
and Imperial Airways were combined by the
government to create BOAC. The gondolier in the
lower right is staring wistfully at a de Havilland 86
biplane, which carried up to twelve passengers
at a speed of 145 m.p.h.

PRECEDING PAGE:

Boeing Stratocruiser

Artist: **Maley**

circa 1950

IMPERIAL AIRWAYS COMFORT ROUTES

The British Air Line

Artist unknown

1930

The pre-war airlines were in competition with
the great ocean liners, then at the height of their
luxury and opulence. The *Imperial Airways Gazette*
of July 1931 describes the clubby appointments of
their airplane cabins, with "large windows, curtained
with choice silks in their tastefully panelled
walls, softly-shaded lights, big chintz covered
armchairs into which one sinks luxuriously,
soft carpets on the floors, and flowers on
tables in front of every seat"

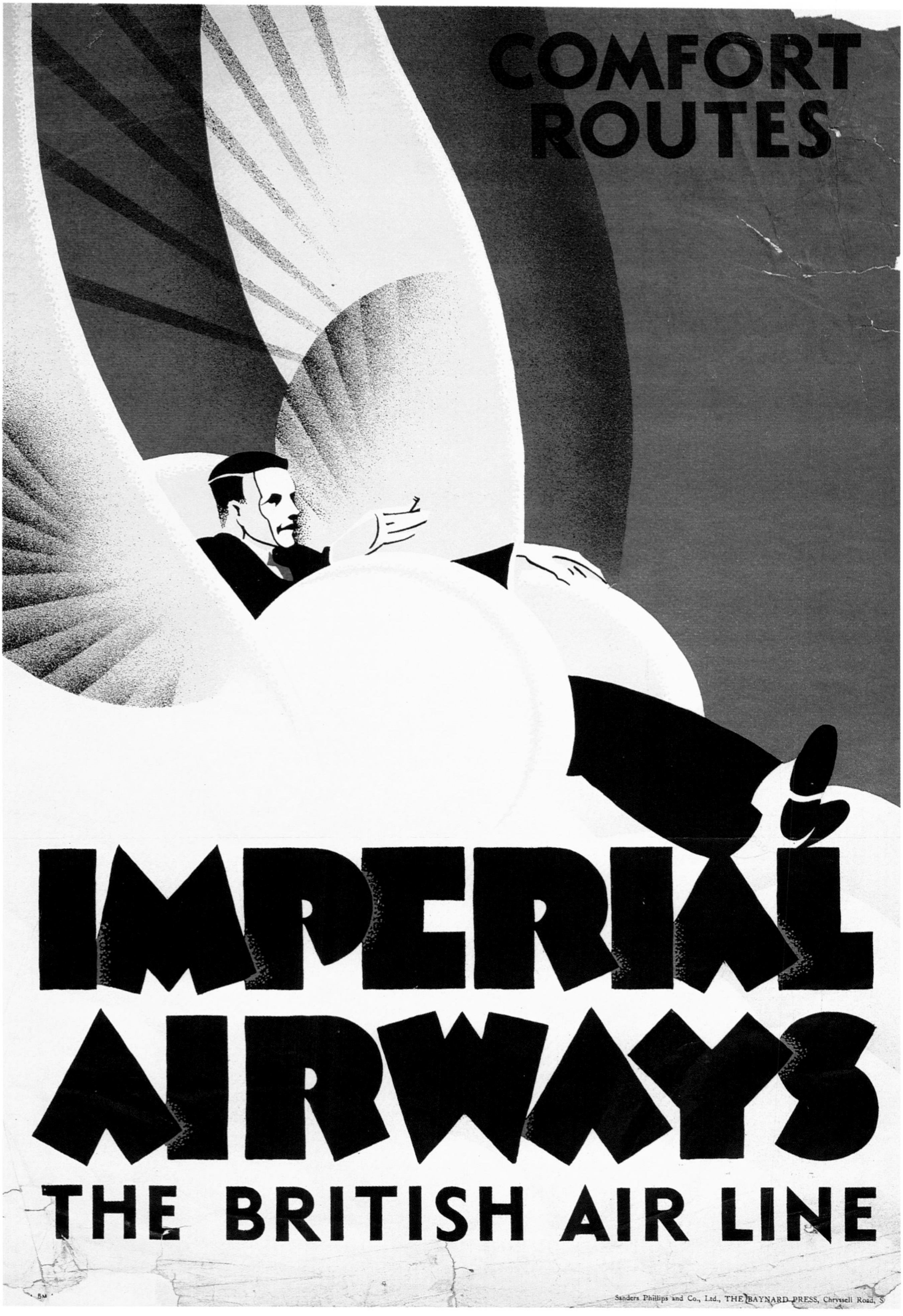
COMFORT
ROUTES
IMPERIAL
AIRWAYS
THE BRITISH AIR LINE
5M
Sanders Phillips and Co., Ltd., THE BAYNARD PRESS, Chryssell Road, S

TRAVEL COMFORTABLY

Imperial Airways and Associated Companies

Europe – Africa – India – China – Australia

Artist: **Fougasse**

1936

Fougasse was the nom de plume of Kenneth Bird,
later editor of *Punch* and one of the most witty and
urbane of twentieth-century commercial artists.
During World War II he created a famous "Careless
Talk Costs Lives" campaign for the Ministry of
Information. By the mid-Thirties Imperial Airways had
helped establish a network of associated companies
in the colonies to handle local traffic; these
included Indian Transcontinental Airways, and
Elders Colonial Airways in West Africa

Travel
comfortably
IMPERIAL
AIRWAYS
AND ASSOCIATED COMPANIES

Europe—Africa—India—China—Australia

PRINTED IN ENGLAND BY M^cCORQUODALE & CO., LTD., LONDON. AND PUBLISHED IN GREAT BRITAIN BY IMPERIAL AIRWAYS LTD., LONDON—IA/P/94—6m—3/36.

LE TOUQUET
ONE FLYING HOUR

Imperial Airways

The Most Comfortable Way

Attributed to Theyre Lee-Elliott

1936

In 1932 the London artist Theyre Lee-Elliott
designed the famous *Speedbird* symbol for
Imperial Airways, and it remained one of the most
well-known and effective company trademarks
anywhere until it was abandoned by the modern
British Airways in 1984. Here it cuts dramatically
across the outline of a human form. The French
coastal town of Le Touquet was popular as a
gambling spot and as a "naughty weekend"
destination. A Sunday excursion price of £3 10s.
included tea at the famous casino

LE TOUQUET
ONE *FLYING* HOUR

IMPERIAL AIRWAYS
THE MOST COMFORTABLE WAY

AUSTRALIA
10½ DAYS
IMPERIAL AIRWAYS
AND ASSOCIATED COMPANIES

Artist: **Albert Brenet**

1935

In 1935, the Imperial Airways ten-and-a-half-day
route from England to Australia represented
tremendous speed: the steamship journey took six
weeks or more. Surprisingly, the only portion of the
route which was not possible by air was between
Paris and Brindisi, since the Italian government would
not allow planes originating in France to fly over its
territory. At Brindisi, passengers boarded a flying
boat for Alexandria and then proceeded by small
landplanes, such as this de Havilland 86, operated
by Qantas on the Singapore–Brisbane run

IMPERIAL AIRWAYS

For Longer Leave in England Fly Home

Inclusive Fares

'No Extras'

Artist: **Theyre Lee-Elliott**

circa 1935

The sleek Speedbird symbol gives an
almost Expressionist third dimension to the map
of Africa, painted in warm "African" colours. The
message is an attempt by the airline to graduate from
novelty or VIP patronage to a regular clientele.
This poster by the Speedbird's inventor,
Theyre Lee-Elliott, was also produced in French,
offering a six-day service once a week from Brussels
to the Congo. A companion poster shows a
Speedbird map of India and Ceylon in red
and blue, with the legend "Home by Air.
Rebate Fares for Serving Officers"

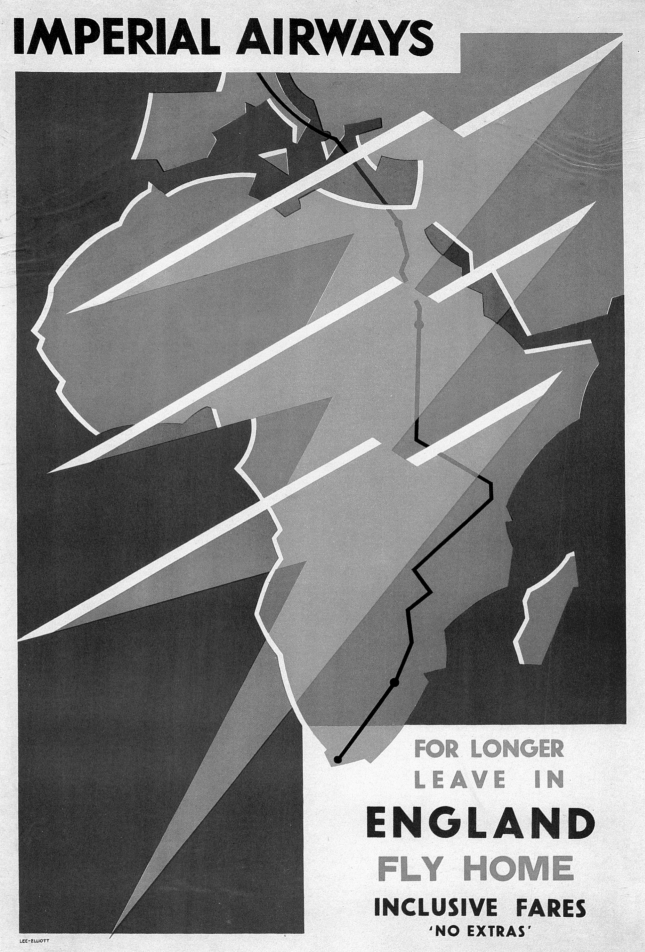

AS THE CROW FLIES — ONLY FASTER!

British Airways

Paris & Scandinavia

See Your Travel Agent

Artist: **Theyre Lee-Elliott**

circa 1935

Lee-Elliott designed this poster, circa 1935,
for the newly formed British Airways, which
specialised in short-haul service to Paris and
Scandinavia. British Airways eventually adopted the
flying lion as its symbol, but the airline
was not in existence long enough to develop a
recognisable trademark with the popularity of the
Imperial Airways Speedbird. However, this soaring
bird and aircraft, together with a stirring
slogan, are effective in conveying a
sense of motion and excitement

BRITISH AIRWAYS

The Most Pleasant Route to Paris

Frequent Services Daily

£6-6-0 Week-End Return

Book Your Seat Here

Artist: **Marshall Thompson**

circa 1936

The shadow of an airplane on the ground
was a popular device in airline posters throughout
the Thirties, Forties and Fifties. While most airline
advertisements of the mid-Thirties projected a
sophisticated image, this one features fresh spring-
like colours. British Airways and Imperial Airways
combined to offer seven daily flights during the
week, and five at weekends, between Croydon
Aerodrome and Le Bourget, in fierce competition
with Air France on the world's most heavily travelled
international air route, the London–Paris service

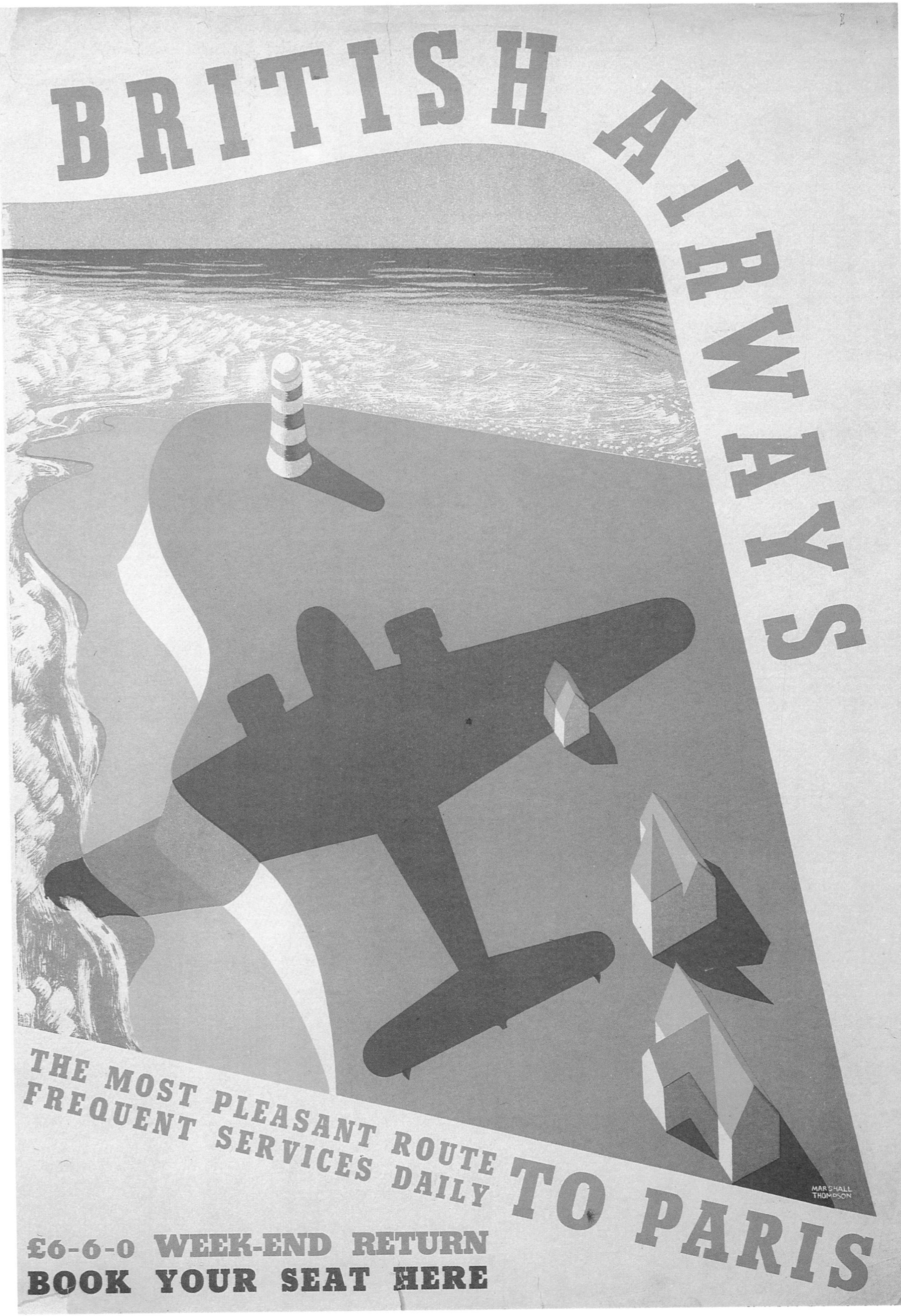
BRITISH AIRWAYS
THE MOST PLEASANT ROUTE
FREQUENT SERVICES DAILY
TO PARIS
£6-6-0 WEEK-END RETURN
BOOK YOUR SEAT HERE
MARSHALL THOMPSON

BY AIR IN COMFORT

To Europe Africa Asia by Imperial Airways

Artist: **Steph Cavallero**

circa 1937

An Art Deco wonder by Steph Cavallero repeats
the theme of comfort and service. The plush armchair
retains its place of prominence in an effort to dispel
memories of the more primitive conditions of the
Twenties, when airplane seats were made of wicker,
for lightness. In this picture, it's cocktail time, and the
two figures look as though they could be waiting for
Gertrude Lawrence to make her entrance. Strangely,
the airplane seems to be pointing down, when it
might more reassuringly be pointing up

INDIA BY IMPERIAL AIRWAYS

Artist: **W.H.A. Constable**

circa 1935

(Also on front cover)

From its formation, in 1924,
one of the roles of Imperial Airways was the
binding together of far-flung parts of the Empire.
A Handley Page 42, the *Hannibal*, (nicknamed the
Flying Banana because of its ungainly shape)
gliding over an Indian city on the banks of a river
expresses the romance of this important
strategic function. The Royal Mail emblem is
displayed on the door of a special compartment
for the storage of mail bags. In 1934 the
government announced plans for the All-Up
Empire Mail scheme, by which letters
for any part of the Empire would
automatically be sent by air

INDIA

BY IMPERIAL
AIRWAYS

IAX/63

PRINTED IN GREAT BRITAIN STUARTS, KINGSWAY HOUSE

BRITISH AIRWAYS LTD

Terminal House · Victoria · London

SLOane 0091

Paris & Scandinavia

Bookings from All Principal Travel Agents

Artist: **Theyre Lee-Elliott**

circa 1937

While Imperial Airways was limited to a Buy British
policy in building its fleet, British Airways took
delivery in 1937 of the latest Lockheed monoplanes
from America, such as the one silhouetted in this
poster by Lee-Elliott. The famous photograph of
Neville Chamberlain returning from Munich in 1938
shows a British Airways Lockheed 14 in the
background. This poster has the slightly unsettling
suggestion of an air raid, with a strong
searchlight illuminating the aircraft

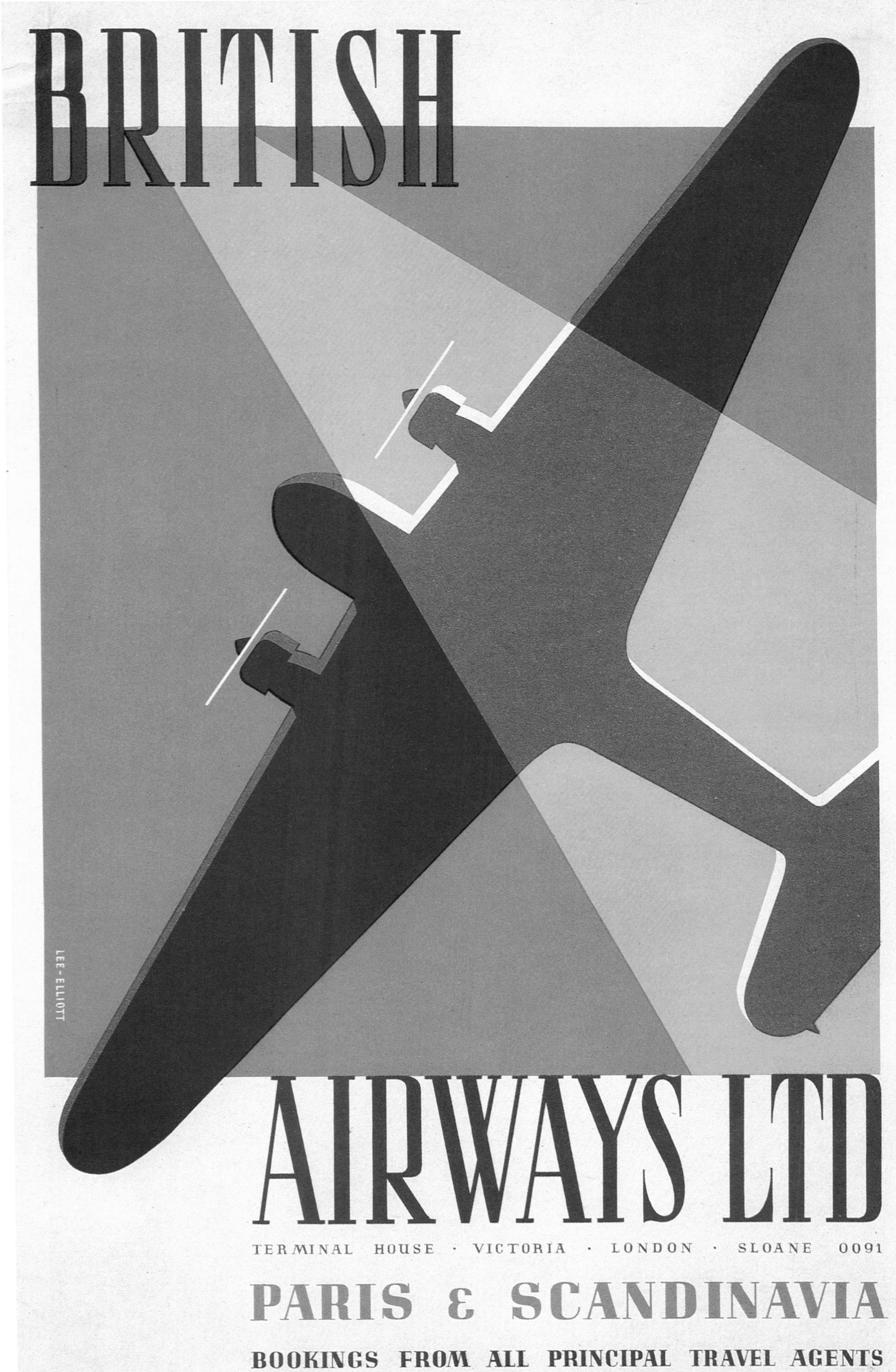
BRITISH
LEE-ELLIOTT
AIRWAYS LTD
TERMINAL HOUSE · VICTORIA · LONDON · SLOANE 0091
PARIS & SCANDINAVIA
BOOKINGS FROM ALL PRINCIPAL TRAVEL AGENTS

**COLOGNE LEIPZIG PRAGUE
VIENNA BUDAPEST**

Weekday Services from London

Imperial Airways Four Engined Air Liners

Designer unknown

1935

Muted, melancholy colours give a *Third Man* effect
to this photographic poster for one of the great
routes through Germany and Central Europe,
a service which stopped forever four years later.
Another version of this poster, printed for the
Imperial Airways Budapest agency, lists a return
fare to London of 630 Hungarian pengoes.
The plane is a de Havilland 86. Before the
introduction of the wheel under the nose
of the aircraft, airplanes sloped sharply
—and, for the passengers, uncomfortably—
backwards prior to take-off

COLOGNE
LEIPZIG
PRAGUE
VIENNA
BUDAPEST

WEEKDAY SERVICES FROM LONDON

IMPERIAL

AIRWAYS

FOUR ENGINED AIR LINERS

PRINTED IN GREAT BRITAIN BY THE SUN ENGRAVING CO., LTD., LONDON, AND PUBLISHED BY IMPERIAL AIRWAYS, LTD., ENGLAND.

**IMPERIAL AIRWAYS AND
ASSOCIATED COMPANIES OPERATE THE
WORLD'S LONGEST AIR ROUTE**

Artist unknown

1936

Another aircraft silhouette, with a globe
to show the Imperial Airways routes, which totalled
almost 20,000 miles. The two long-haul Empire
services divided at Alexandria—one heading south
through Africa for a further six days to Johannesburg,
the other travelling east through Palestine
and the Gulf through to India and Australia.
By 1936 South African Airways operated local
services from Johannesburg, extending
the route to Cape Town

Imperial Airways

and Associated Companies

Operate the world's longest air route

**IMPERIAL AIRWAYS TO ENGLAND
FOR THE CORONATION**

The quick way to the world's greatest event.
The weeks you save can be added to your
time in England

Artist unknown

1937

A very traditional style is evident in this poster
for the last full-scale imperial coronation, of 1937.
The central figure changed — from King Edward VIII to
King George VI — during preparations for the
coronation, but the date of May 12th remained the
same. Another version of this popular poster lists the
full season's calendar of festive events, beginning
with the Ideal Home Exhibition on April 22nd, and
ending with the Derby, June 2nd. The message is not
one of comfort and luxury en route, but rather of
the increased holiday time at the destination

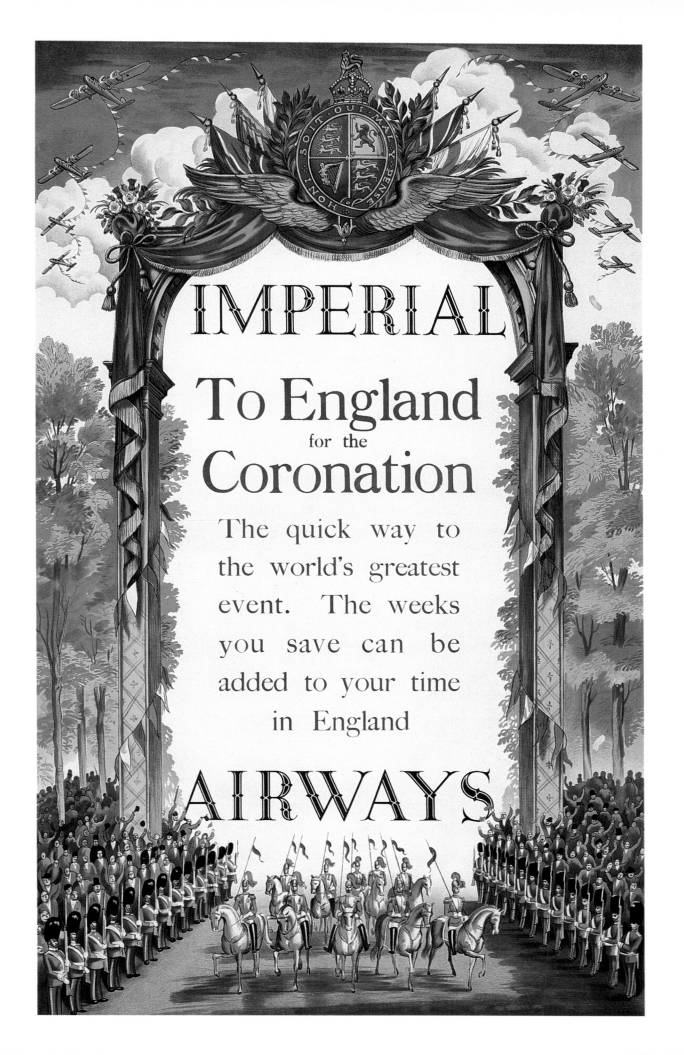

EVERY IMPERIAL AIR LINER HAS
4 ENGINES FOR SECURITY

Imperial Airways in 1937 carried over 70,000
passengers and flew over 6,000,000 miles

Artist: **V.L. Danvers**

1938

This 1938 poster was printed in several
languages, including French, German and Italian.
Passengers are shown boarding a Handley Page 42,
the *Heracles*, while the pilot and co-pilot, all scrubbed
and smiling, are visible through the windscreen.
One of their duties on take-off was to lower the
Civil Air Ensign through a hatch in the cockpit roof.
The HP-42 was one of the most luxurious airplanes in
the sky and was a mainstay of Imperial Airways'
famous Silver Wing service between London and
Paris. By 1938, however, this stately aircraft looked
very old-fashioned next to the new British Airways
Lockheed monoplanes (See Page 35)

EVERY IMPERIAL AIR LINER HAS

4 ENGINES
FOR SECURITY

IMPERIAL AIRWAYS
in 1937 carried over 70,000 passengers
and flew over 6,000,000 miles

BERMUDA IN 5 HOURS

Pan American Airways

Imperial Airways

Artist: **P.G. Lawler**

1937

This five-hour flight was from New York,
and was run as a joint service with Pan American,
beginning in June 1937. Imperial's service would not
have been with the type of craft whose shadow is
visible here, but rather with the Empire flying boat
Cavalier, which was specially fitted with a
long-range capability for the 800-mile voyage.
There were two flights a week during the summer
season, one a week in the winter. The *Cavalier* was
lost en route in January 1939, ending Imperial
Airways' participation in this service

FLY THERE BY WILSON AIRWAYS

Artist: **Stagg**

circa 1935

Wilson Airways, based in Nairobi,
was one of the most colourful private airline
companies operating in the colonies.
Founded in 1929 by Mrs. F.K. Wilson, it provided
mail and transportation to up-country settlements,
also spotting herds of lions and elephants for
hunting safaris. Mrs. Wilson and her pilot,
Captain M.C.P. Mostert, pioneered air links in
East Africa, beginning in 1930 with a route survey
from Nairobi to Johannesburg. The next year they
carved a route across Africa, from Zanzibar to Dakar
via the Belgian Congo, and by 1932 they were
connecting with Imperial Airways flights into
Nairobi with service to Mombasa, Zanzibar and
Dar es Salaam. Wilson Airways went into
liquidation in 1940, and with it ended
one of the great bush airlines

FLY THERE BY

WILSON AIRWAYS

28 HYDROAVIONS TYPE 'EMPIRE'

Vitesse: 320 Kilomètres Heure

Imperial Airways

Europe Afrique Indes Extrême-Orient

Australie

Artist: **Albert Brenet**

1937

The RMA *Canopus* was the first of the
twenty-eight long-haul flying boats which
Imperial Airways bought from Short Brothers almost
straight from the drawing board in 1937. Here it is
shown in splendid repose at a quayside seadrome.
The Empire class flying boats were the first of the
luxury type, and variations of this design were
in service with BOAC until 1950. The flying boat
quickly became the mainstay of the long-haul routes
to Africa, India and Australia. Planned for elegance
and comfort, each one had a two-level
interior and a promenade deck

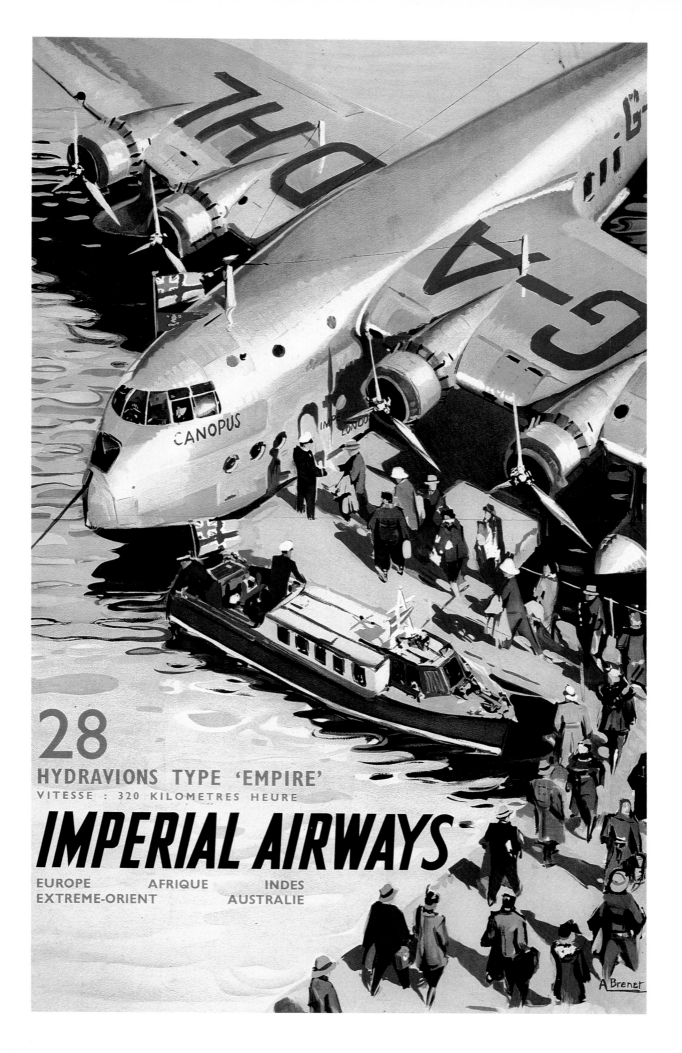

28 HYDRAVIONS 'EMPIRE' NEUFS

À Vitesse de 320 Kilomètres à l'Heure

Imperial Airways

Europe Afrique Inde Extrême Orient

Australie

Artist: **Albert Brenet**

1937

Another poster advertising the fleet
of Short Empire class flying boats, by Albert Brenet,
a Parisian artist whose bold conception is well suited
to the poster format. This poster appeared in several
languages, including Arabic and Hebrew. There is the
possibility of slight menace in these swarming
aircraft, and indeed two years later the flying
boat proved highly adaptable to war work

THE FORTIES

IT'S A SMALLER WORLD

BY SPEEDBIRD

FLY BOAC

Artist: **Beverley Pick**

circa 1948

The national airline was renamed British
Overseas Airways Corporation with effect from 1940,
and the new name emerged into the world of
commercial flying after World War II. (BOAC was
formally disbanded in 1974 to become part of the
current British Airways.) The sleek Speedbird symbol
was more prominent than ever in the BOAC era, and
even the name *Speedbird* was used as a synonym
for the airline. The creator of this poster,
Beverley Pick, worked extensively for BOAC
during the late Forties and Fifties.
In addition to posters, he designed aircraft
livery, interiors and window displays for
BOAC offices in London and overseas

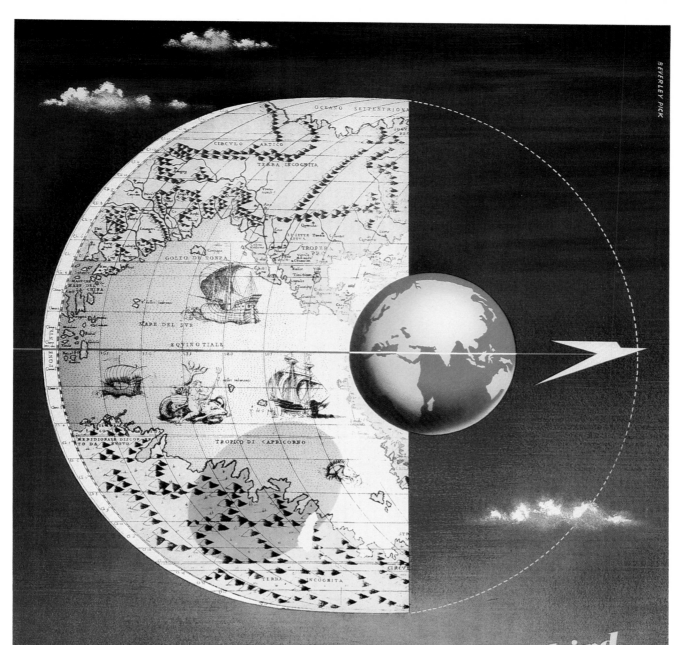

*it's a **smaller** world by Speedbird*

fly **B·O·A·C**

BRITISH OVERSEAS AIRWAYS CORPORATION IN ASSOCIATION WITH Q.E.A., S.A.A. AND T.E.A.L.

IN AUSTRALIAN SKIES . . .
A NEW CONSTELLATION
QANTAS EMPIRE AIRWAYS
The "Kangaroo" Service Sydney–London
In Association with B.O.A.C.

Artist unknown

circa 1947

In 1947, Qantas became a wholly Australian-owned
airline, with the purchase of BOAC's shares in the
company. In December of that year Qantas began
service to London with four Lockheed Constellations.
These American long-range aircraft were some
of the most beautiful and graceful planes ever built.
They cut travel time between London and Sydney
from seven down to four days, and meant the
beginning of the end of the flying boat

IN AUSTRALIAN SKIES...
A New Constellation

Qantas

EMPIRE AIRWAYS

THE "KANGAROO" SERVICE SYDNEY—LONDON
In Association with B.O.A.C.

FLY THE ATLANTIC BY BOAC

Stratocruiser Speedbird

Artist: **Abram Games**

1949

The necessities of war demanded the
development of the transatlantic passenger service,
a route almost entirely over water and hampered
by exceedingly harsh weather conditions.
Experimental flights had been made in the Thirties,
but it was the North Atlantic Return Ferry Service, for
pilots delivering bombers to Britain in 1940, that
made regular transatlantic passenger flights a reality.
With the resumption of commercial flying in 1946,
the North Atlantic was no longer a formidable barrier.
Indeed, it was the prestige route of the future.
In Abram Games's 1949 poster, Speedbirds glide
effortlessly between Britain and America as the map
of the world symbolically becomes smaller

A. GAMES
FLY THE ATLANTIC BY
B·O·A·C
ATLANTIC OCEAN
Stratocruiser
Speedbird
BRITISH OVERSEAS AIRWAYS CORPORATION IN ASSOCIATION WITH QANTAS EMPIRE AIRWAYS LTD., SOUTH AFRICAN AIRWAYS, TASMAN EMPIRE AIRWAYS LTD.

FLY TO BRITAIN BY BOAC

Artist: **Clive Uptton**

circa 1948

Britain's post-war transition from the centre
of the Empire to a tourist destination is evident in this
poster by Clive Uptton, circa 1948.
Most of the tourists came from America.
The Lockheed Constellation, seen hovering
over Hyde Park Corner, could have left New York
at 5.05 p.m. and would be arriving in London at
2.45 p.m. the next day, having stopped in Gander,
Newfoundland, and Shannon; an alternative route
stopped at Gander and Prestwick, adding
only half an hour on to the flight

FLY QEA and BOAC

Qantas Empire Airways in Parallel

with British Overseas Airways Corporation

Two Routes via the Kangaroo Service

By Constellation or Flying Boat

at the Same Fare

Artist unknown

circa 1947

From 1947 until the end of flying boat service
in 1950, Lockheed Constellations and Short
Sandringhams plied the London–Sydney route in
parallel. The long-range Constellation landplane
called in at only seven places, exactly half the number
of stops as the flying boat service. The flying boat in
this poster, serial number G-A GKY, came to an
ignominious end: sold to the tiny Aquila Airways in
1948 for holiday flights from Britain to Madeira,
it crashed on take-off from Southampton
in January 1953 and sank while it was
being towed in for repairs

FLY
Q·E·A and B·O·A·C
QANTAS EMPIRE AIRWAYS IN PARALLEL WITH BRITISH OVERSEAS AIRWAYS CORPORATION
LONDON
MARSEILLES
AUGUSTA
CASTEL BENITO
CAIRO
BASRA
BAHREIN
KARACHI
CALCUTTA
RANGOON
SINGAPORE
SOURABAYA
DARWIN
BOWEN
SYDNEY
AUCKLAND
G-AGKY
TWO ROUTES VIA THE KANGAROO SERVICE
BY CONSTELLATION OR FLYING BOAT
AT THE SAME FARE

BRITISH OVERSEAS AIRWAYS

The World's Best Known Signpost at Karachi, India, tells the story of B.O.A.C.:
Wings Over the World

IN SOUTH AMERICA TO-MORROW

British South American Airways

Artist: **Gwynn**

circa 1946

British South American Airways was a subsidiary
of BOAC, established directly after the war and
disbanded in 1949. The overnight service to
South America left London twice a week at noon and
made the South Atlantic crossing that same night
from Bathurst, in the Gambia, to Natal, on the
east coast of Brazil. Passengers were
in Rio de Janeiro by 3.15 p.m.

in SOUTH AMERICA
TO-MORROW
BRITISH
SOUTH AMERICAN
AIRWAYS
GWYNN

BOAC
IT'S A SMALL WORLD BY SPEEDBIRD

Artist unknown

1946

The Short Sandringham was one of the last of
the flying boat types in service. Larger than the
Empire class flying boats of 1937, its two-level
interior, divided into cabins, preserved the luxurious
feeling of sea travel. In the late Forties, the flying boat
was living on borrowed time, enjoying a brief Indian
summer due to the shortage of new aircraft following
World War II. But even in this 1946 poster,
the swifter Constellation has appeared in the
background, ready to eclipse the flying boat
forever within four years

B·O·A·C

it's a small world by

SPEEDBIRD

BRITISH OVERSEAS AIRWAYS CORPORATION IN ASSOCIATION WITH
QANTAS EMPIRE AIRWAYS · SOUTH AFRICAN AIRWAYS · TASMAN EMPIRE AIRWAYS

TASMAN SKYWAY

TEAL

Tasman Empire Airways Limited
Head Office Auckland New Zealand
in association with Q.E.A., B.O.A.C.
and B.C.P.A.

Artist: **William Haythorn Thwaite**

circa 1947

Tasman Empire Airways, the precursor of
today's Air New Zealand, was established in 1940
to provide service between New Zealand and
Australia across the Tasman Sea, a nine-hour journey.
Its flying boats extended the London–Sydney
Kangaroo Route as far as Auckland. In this poster
by the Auckland artist Haythorn Thwaite, a carved
Maori gateway stands in the foreground, with the
Sydney Harbour Bridge (in the days before the
Opera House) visible across the water

TASMAN *Skyway*

TEAL

TASMAN ★ EMPIRE ★ AIRWAYS ★ LIMITED

HEAD OFFICE   AUCKLAND   NEW ZEALAND   in association with Q

W. HAYTHORN-THWAITE LIMITED

**TO NAIROBI BY BOAC — AND THEN BY
EAST AFRICAN AIRWAYS CORPORATION
TO ALL PARTS OF EAST AFRICA**

Artist unknown

circa 1946

An African spear is decorated with scenes from
colonial life and a sketch of the new airline's services,
which were centred in Nairobi. East African Airways
was established in 1946 by the British-run
governments of Kenya, Uganda, Tanganyika and
Zanzibar, following many of the routes established
by the legendary Wilson Airways (See Page 47).
As part of British policy to rationalise air
communications in Africa, Central African Airways
was also formed at this time, to serve
the Rhodesias and Nyasaland

TO NAIROBI BY B·O·A·C· AND THEN BY

EAST

AFRICAN

AIRWAYS

CORPORATION

NAIROBI

TO ALL PARTS OF EAST AFRICA

FLY WITH THE STARS
TO SOUTH & CENTRAL AMERICA AND
THE WEST INDIES

By Star Liners of

British South American Airways

Artist unknown

circa 1947

A sultry scene from this short-lived
British airline of the late Forties.
The fortnightly London–Caribbean service began
in September 1946, crossing the Atlantic between
the Azores and Bermuda, and continuing on to
Kingston and Caracas. In July 1949, BSAA was
merged with BOAC. The mysterious disappearance
of BSAA aircraft on this route in 1948
and 1949 fuelled legends of the treacherous
"Bermuda Triangle"

Fly with the Stars

TO SOUTH & CENTRAL AMERICA
AND THE WEST INDIES
BY STAR LINERS OF

BRITISH SOUTH AMERICAN AIRWAYS

BOAC SPEEDBIRD ROUTES

. . . ACROSS THE WORLD

Britain—Australia by the Kangaroo Service

In Association with QEA

(Also on back cover)

Artist: **Harold Forster**

1946

One of a series of posters painted by Harold Forster
for BOAC immediately following World War II.
This example shows an Australian rancher;
others have an Indian in a turban, a Chinese farmer
and an African Bushman scanning the sky in a similar
pose, with their respective routes highlighted
on the map. The word *Speedbird* as well as the
symbol itself was used increasingly in
this period to signify BOAC

QEA KANGAROO SERVICE

London–Sydney by Constellation

Qantas Empire Airways in Parallel

with British Overseas Airways Corporation

Artist unknown

circa 1949

The Lockheed Constellation, with its slightly
humped back and three distinctive tailfins,
was one of the most graceful aircraft ever designed.
Gone is the generous two-level accommodation of
the Short flying boats (See Page 67): the interior
of the Constellation resembles the airliners of today.
Constellations were also some of the first commercial
aircraft to have pressurised cabins.
The advantage of speed proved to be more of an
attraction than elegance, and these long-range
landplanes almost halved the journey time
between Britain and Australia

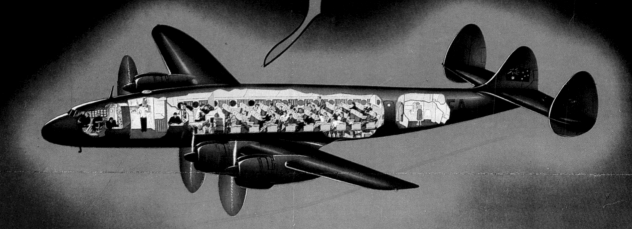

Q·E·A

KANGAROO   SERVICE

London-Sydney
BY CONSTELLATION

QANTAS EMPIRE AIRWAYS IN PARALLEL WITH BRITISH OVERSEAS AIRWAYS CORPORATION

THROUGHOUT THE CARIBBEAN
BRITISH WEST INDIAN AIRWAYS

Artist: **Daphne Padden**

circa 1949

Formed in response to the collapse of
communications in wartime, BWIA was created in
1940 by the New Zealander Lowell Yerex, a charter
operator who was instrumental in the development
of air service in the Caribbean and Central America.
Owned in turn by British South American Airways and
BOAC, it was purchased by the government of
Trinidad and Tobago in 1961. Flying boats continue
to be used in parts of the Caribbean even today in
remote islands without proper landing strips.
Another advantage of the flying boat is the possibility
of free landing and storage in lagoons such
as the one in this poster

THROUGHOUT THE
CARIBBEAN
BRITISH WEST INDIAN
AIRWAYS
BWIA
BWIA
DAPHNE PADDEN

FLY TO BRITAIN BY BOAC

British Overseas Airways Corporation in
Association with Qantas Empire Airways,
South African Airways,
Tasman Empire Airways Limited

Artist: **Chater**

1948

Britain's timeless beauty became an increasingly
popular theme of BOAC posters in the Forties and
Fifties, as part of the national campaign to
earn foreign exchange through tourism.
BOAC's associated companies in Australia,
South Africa and New Zealand were listed on posters
until the late 1950s, by which time these
Commonwealth airlines had become fierce
competitors of BOAC

FLY TO SOUTH AFRICA BY BOAC AND SAA

Artist unknown

circa 1947

After World War II, BOAC and South African Airways
operated a parallel service between London and
Johannesburg. SAA's route, using American-built
Douglas DC-4 landplanes, took only thirty-three
hours, leaving London Airport (Heathrow) three
times a week at 8.0 a.m. and arriving in Johannesburg
at 7.05 the next evening. BOAC's Solent flying boat
service took five days, but offered spectacular
views of Luxor and Victoria Falls

FLY TO
SOUTH
AFRICA

BY B·O·A·C AND S·A·A

BRITISH OVERSEAS AIRWAYS CORPORATION IN ASSOCIATION WITH SOUTH AFRICAN AIRWAYS, QANTAS EMPIRE AIRWAYS LTD., TASMAN EMPIRE AIRWAYS LTD.

FLY TO THE FAR EAST

BOAC

Artist: **Rowland Hilder**

circa 1948

The transport of the past and of the future
are both pictured in Hong Kong in this atmospheric
poster by Rowland Hilder. A Lockheed Constellation
soars overhead, while a Short S-25 Sandringham
flying boat rests among colourful craft in Victoria
Harbour. The Sandringham in this picture, serial
number G-AKCR, was named the *St. Andrew*, and
was sold by the airline in 1950, the last
year of BOAC's flying boat service

FLY TO THE FAR EAST

B·O·A·C

BRITISH OVERSEAS AIRWAYS CORPORATION IN ASSOCIATION WITH Q.E.A., S.A.A. AND T.E.A.L.

FLY TO SOUTH AMERICA BY BOAC

British Overseas Airways Corporation

Artist: **Laurence Keeble**

1949

This BOAC poster reflects the demise
of the post-war British South American Airways,
which was absorbed by BOAC in July 1949. The South
Atlantic route was clearly not profitable enough to
support the six competing airlines which were
offering parallel service by 1948. As the destination,
rather than the concept of flying, became a more
important selling point in the Forties and Fifties,
the airplane itself became less prominent on the
posters. Here it is absent altogether

FLY TO SOUTH AMERICA

BY

B·O·A·C

BRITISH OVERSEAS AIRWAYS CORPORATION

VUELE AL MAR CARIBE POR BOAC

Artist: **Aubrey Rix**

1949–50

This Spanish version of a 1949 poster for
BOAC's Caribbean service was displayed in the
airline's South American offices.
The woman in the picture is Audrey White,
the famous Rix Girl, depicted by Aubrey Rix on the
covers of *Woman's Own* from 1947 to 1951.
To many she symbolised the ideal British
young woman of the post-war period — informal,
full of pep, and well supplied with handsome young
men hovering eagerly in the background

Vuele al Mar Caribe
POR B·O·A·C

BCPA LEADS THE WAY ACROSS THE
PACIFIC WITH THE "PRESSURISED" DC-6

Now Flying the "Southern Cross" Route

Vancouver · San Francisco · Honolulu · Fiji

Auckland · Sydney

British Commonwealth Pacific Airlines Ltd.

Artist unknown

circa 1949

Another short-lived post-war airline
was British Commonwealth Pacific Airlines, formed
in 1946 as an Australian–New Zealand–British
partnership. Its island-hopping service across the
South Pacific from San Francisco to Sydney,
via Honolulu, Fiji and Auckland, was absorbed
by Qantas when the two airlines merged in 1954.
The addition of this pioneering route to the
Australian company's network helped Qantas
to become the world's first airline to offer a
scheduled service completely round the
world, in January 1958

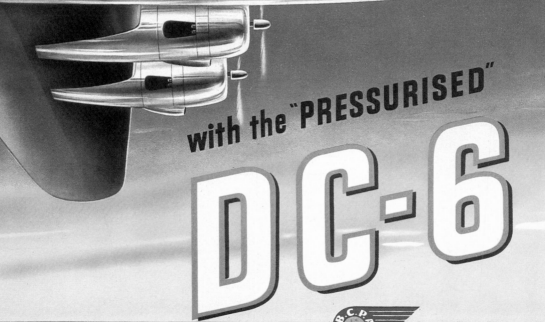

T̲H̲E̲ FIFTIES

FLY TO BRITAIN FOR FESTIVAL YEAR

BOAC

Artist: **Abram Games**

1950

Called by its organisers
"A Tonic to the Nation", the 1951 Festival
of Britain was the landmark event of the post-war
period. Abram Games, who has had one of the
longest and most successful careers of any British
commercial artist, was the designer of the Festival of
Britain symbol—a triangulated star topped with the
head of Britannia. In this 1950 poster, the Speedbird,
which first appeared in the Thirties and came
to be synonymous with BOAC in the Forties,
now becomes the focal point of the
picture in its own right

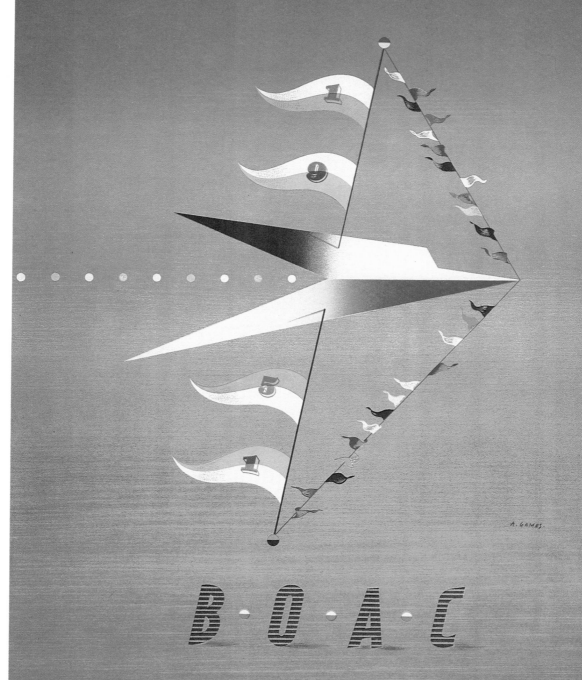

FLY TO BRITAIN FOR FESTIVAL YEAR

A. GAMES.

B·O·A·C

BRITISH OVERSEAS AIRWAYS CORPORATION IN ASSOCIATION WITH QANTAS EMPIRE AIRWAYS LTD., SOUTH AFRICAN AIRWAYS, TASMAN EMPIRE AIRWAYS LTD.

FLY BY BOAC

USA

Artists: **Dick Negus and Philip Sharland**

1954

A rare BOAC venture into the atom age
design world of the Fifties is seen in this 1954 poster
by Dick Negus and Philip Sharland. Neither an aircraft
nor the Speedbird are present here, only the angular
excitement of New York, in a flattened transistorised
view of Times Square. Negus and Sharland produced
a series of posters for BOAC, all featuring
striking Day-Glo images (See Page 97)

fly by BOAC

u·s·a

HOTEL

BRITISH OVERSEAS AIRWAYS CORPORATION IN ASSOCIATION WITH QANTAS EMPIRE AIRWAYS LIMITED · SOUTH AFRICAN AIRWAYS · TASMAN EMPIRE AIRWAYS LIMITED

FLY BY BOAC

GREAT BRITAIN

Artists: **Dick Negus and Philip Sharland**

1954

The companion poster to the previous plate
showing New York, this atom age design presents a
stylised view of Piccadilly Circus, with familiar
London touches, such as the red Routemaster bus
and the London Transport Underground sign. This
Fifties concept of England is a departure from
the nostalgic changeless image presented in most
airline posters featuring Britain as a tourist
destination (See Pages 59 and 81)

fly by B·O·A·C
IME
TO
REST
CIGARETTES
B·O·A·C
fly BOAC to all six continents
Great
Britain
KEEP
LEFT

FLY TO AUSTRALIA
SO NEAR BY BOAC & QANTAS

Artist unknown

circa 1950

Australia is presented here as a holiday
destination, a place to find summer in the middle
of the British winter. The mood is sunny, but also
slightly sophisticated, with the woman's modish
spectacles, the intriguing green beverage in her glass
and the New Look fashion magazine lying on the
table. The distinctive Constellation, flying in the
upper right, displays the Qantas red stripe

BOAC COMET JETLINER

HASTEN AT LEISURE

Artist: **Ken Bromfield**

1952

This poster by Ken Bromfield announces
BOAC's de Havilland Comet. It was the world's first
jet airliner, and was inaugurated in 1952.
Called by the air historian R.E.G. Davies
the "Magnificent False Start" to the jet age, this
triumph of British engineering went sour in 1954
when, after two Comets broke apart in mid-air
because of metal fatigue, the aircraft's certificate
of air-worthiness was withdrawn. By the time a
perfected Comet 4 was introduced in 1958,
America's Boeing 707 had firmly taken over as the
leader in the long-haul jet market

FLY TO EUROPE BY BOAC

Artist unknown

1952

The model in this appealing picture
resembles Audrey Hepburn, in a rare BOAC poster
showing European destinations. These were, strictly
speaking, the territory of BEA. Paris is noticeably
absent from the cities listed: Frankfurt, Zurich, Rome,
Madrid and Lisbon were all transit stops on BOAC
long-haul routes. The fresh vivid colours of the
flowers are particularly lovely in this picture,
as is the woman's delicate cape

Fly to Europe by
B·O·A·C

FRANKFURT LONDON ZURICH ROME MADRID LISBON

BRITISH OVERSEAS AIRWAYS CORPORATION IN ASSOCIATION WITH QANTAS EMPIRE AIRWAYS LTD., SOUTH AFRICAN AIRWAYS AND TASMAN EMPIRE AIRWAYS LTD.

SALES—THROUGH THE AIR—WITH
THE GREATEST OF EASE
BOAC

British Overseas Airways Corporation

Artist: **M.P.H.**

1952

Exports and foreign exchange were Britain's
two overwhelming needs in the early Fifties.
Businessmen were some of the few British residents
who were allowed to carry more than £50 out of the
country. Significantly, the names of BOAC's
associated companies in the Commonwealth, who
had become stiff competitors, are not mentioned in
this export-oriented poster from 1952. A slightly
poignant feature in this clever play on words
is the style of the briefcase itself—looking
more appropriate to a headmaster than
an international tycoon

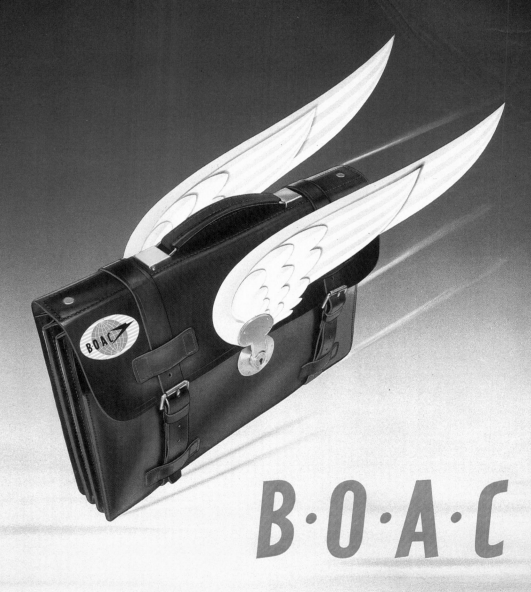

SALES-THROUGH THE AIR-
WITH THE GREATEST OF EASE-

B·O·A·C

FLY TO USA BY BOAC

Artist unknown

1950

A supremely evocative poster from 1950
depicts a rainy night in the New York of *Guys 'n' Dolls*,
with huge glistening American cars and the
distinctive New York policeman. The aircraft flying
past the skyscrapers, in the upper right, is the Boeing
Stratocruiser, recognisable from its bulbous nose.
The introduction of BOAC's Stratocruiser Monarch
Service in 1949 transferred the Constellation
Mayflower Service to second-class status. The two
aircraft had roughly the same speed and range,
but the Stratocruiser was the prestige airliner
of the day, with a cocktail bar and lounge on
a lower deck reached by a spiral staircase

FLY TO U·S·A BY

B·O·A·C

AUSTRALIA

FLY THERE BY BOAC AND QANTAS

Artist: **Hayes**

1953

Australia and bathing beauties were firmly
linked in posters of the Forties and Fifties, but never
more appealingly than in this 1953 picture by Hayes.
Sunshine and health radiate not just from this Marilyn
Monroe lookalike, but from her surfboard as well.
Another bathing beauty poster, from 1949, carried
the headline "Come On In! Australia Has Everything",
and then proceeded to depict an unusual
combination of attractions—horse racing,
skiing, fishing and theatres

FLY BY BOAC

USA

Artist: **Xenia**

1952

Xenia was a popular *Punch* artist of the
Forties and Fifties, and she created a series of posters
for BOAC in 1952 and 1953. Each was designed like a
postage stamp. This example shows Central Park—
bright, chic, carefree, and very much unlike austerity
England where the luxuries of life, and many of its
necessities, were still subject to rationing.
Other posters in Xenia's series showed South
Africa, India, and South America

FLY BOAC

CANADA

Attributed to Aldo Cosomati

1953

A poster from a 1952–53 series displays a cartoon
quality, and the message is quite abstract. Aircraft are
missing completely, and so is the Speedbird.
Beckoning us to Canada is not some attractive local
scene, but a local type—this slightly wary
looking Indian. The series was printed in
a silk-screen process, with strong Day-Glo
colours on a velvety matt blue

Fly B·O·A·C

CANADA

BRITISH OVERSEAS AIRWAYS CORPORATION IN ASSOCIATION WITH QANTAS EMPIRE AIRWAYS LIMITED · SOUTH AFRICAN AIRWAYS · TASMAN EMPIRE AIRWAYS LIMITED

AUSTRALIA

FLY THERE BY BOAC & QANTAS

Attributed to Aldo Cosomati

1953

In another poster by the same artist,
a cricketer is very skilfully superimposed on a
map of Australia, the green pitch filling in Victoria and
most of New South Wales. The USA poster in this
series continues a sporting theme, showing a very
graceful baseball player swinging a bat; the
poster for Pakistan depicts a charming
and amiable green-eyed tiger

AUSTRALIA

FLY THERE BY

B·O·A·C & QANTAS

FLY TO CEYLON BY BOAC

Artist: **Frank Wootton**

1951

In an immensely attractive village scene
by Frank Wootton, a doyen of aviation artists, a
wooden-wheeled oxcart is pulled along a dusty road
in Ceylon. The airplane is a Handley Page Hermes, the
first British pressurised aircraft built after the war.
Phased out of use with the introduction of Comet jets
in 1952, these sixty-eight-passenger airliners were
brought back into service when the Comets were
suddenly withdrawn two years later

FLY TO CEYLON BY

B·O·A·C

BRITISH OVERSEAS AIRWAYS CORPORATION IN ASSOCIATION WITH QANTAS EMPIRE AIRWAYS LIMITED · SOUTH AFRICAN AIRWAYS · TAS—— EMPIRE AIRWAYS LIMITED

FLY THE ROLLS-ROYCE WAY TO LONDON

BRITISH EUROPEAN AIRWAYS VISCOUNT

Rolls-Royce Propeller Turbines

Artist: **Frank Wootton**

circa 1953

The turbo-prop Vickers Viscount,
powered with Rolls-Royce engines, was in large
measure responsible for the enormous growth of
BEA, the post-war British European and domestic
airline. In a turbo-prop, the propellers are driven
by a jet engine, which was an important stage
in the transition from propeller to jet power.
In this era of British technical innovations which
included the Comet and the turbo-prop, British
engineering was synonymous with success.
This poster by Frank Wootton links a fine aircraft with
the universally respected Rolls-Royce motor car

FLY TO BERMUDA
BY BOAC

Artist unknown

circa 1958

The delights of Bermuda are seen through
an open window, but the modes of transport
depicted are sailing boat and horsecart. In 1954,
because of the shortage of aircraft following the
withdrawal of the Comets, BOAC had suspended
direct service to South America, including Bermuda.
Passengers flew to New York or Baltimore and then
changed airlines to complete their journey. In 1958
London to Bermuda service was resumed, as a stop
on the route to Barbados, Trinidad and Caracas

FLY TO BERMUDA

BY B·O·A·C

BRITISH OVERSEAS AIRWAYS CORPORATION

PRINTED IN ENGLAND THE BAYNARD PRESS

FLY BY BOAC

USA/CANADA

Artist: **Laban**

1956

It is unusual for the USA and Canada to appear
on the same poster, as they did in this 1956 picture
by Laban. Both destinations are abstracted—
the USA with a green cartoon skyscraper, and Canada
symbolised by this endearing creature with Day-Glo
paws who looks dazzled, as though surprised by a
sudden flash bulb

fly by  B·O·A·C

U·S·A | Canada

BRITISH OVERSEAS AIRWAYS CORPORATION IN ASSOCIATION WITH QANTAS EMPIRE AIRWAYS LIMITED · SOUTH AFRICAN AIRWAYS · TASMAN EMPIRE AIRWAYS LIMITED

56 / 606

Printed in Great Britain

BOAC/QANTAS
AUSTRALIA/NEW ZEALAND

Artist: **Laban**

1956

Another in Laban's charming series,
with Day-Glo colours backed with a Populuxe purple.
A smiling kangaroo, arms crossed complacently,
carries a koala bear in its pouch. In the background
is the Sydney Harbour Bridge, still without the
Opera House, which appeared on the skyline in
the next decade. A third poster by Laban
shows an equally spirited group of dogs,
representing the countries of Europe

B·O·A·C
QANTAS

Australia
NEW ZEALAND

BRITISH OVERSEAS AIRWAYS CORPORATION · QANTAS EMPIRE AIRWAYS LIMITED · TASMAN EMPIRE AIRWAYS LIMITED

FLY TO THE RHODESIAS BY BOAC

Artist: **Frank Wootton**

1951

Strong shimmering colours characterise
this picture by Frank Wootton, as a stately antelope
is surprised in the wild at the edge of the jungle.
BOAC passengers to Salisbury, Rhodesia, connected
with Central African Airways for Lusaka,
Dar es Salaam and Nairobi. This poster is dated 1951,
and the ill-fated Comet—the pioneer jet airliner,
shown in the background—entered service the
following year. The world's first commercial
jet route was on BOAC's London–Africa
run, to Johannesburg

FLY TO CANADA BY BOAC

Artist: **Chater**

circa 1952

The timeless beauty of the Canadian wilds
is lovingly shown in this picture from the early Fifties.
The emphasis is on the destination, not the journey—
in contrast to the Cunard Line slogan of the same
period, "Getting There is Half the Fun." No airplane
shatters the peace and calm of this lake or inlet,
with the horse and mail boat the only apparent
links with the outside world

Fly to Canada

BY
B·O·A·C

FLY TO THE CARIBBEAN BY BOAC

Artist: **Frank Wootton**

1951

Frank Wootton is equally adept at depicting
aircraft with rigorous accuracy and showing enticing
local scenes in imaginative detail—as in this
West Indian market overflowing with exotic fruits and
vegetables. Always, his colours are warm and
appetising. The tourists, although dressed in white,
have a glow which puts them in harmony with
the rich tones around them

FLY TO AUSTRALIA BY BOAC & QANTAS

Artist: **Frank Wootton**

1950

The aircraft is the focus of this
1950 poster by Frank Wootton, which glories in the
graceful form of the Lockheed Constellation.
The BOAC Speedbird is displayed on one
of the aircraft's distinctive tailfins, which were
added to the design for stability. The last of the BOAC
flying boats went out of service in December 1950,
leaving this long-range landplane supreme
on the London–Australia route

FLY TO AUSTRALIA BY
B·O·A·C & QANTAS

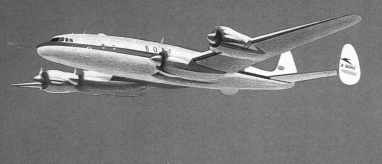

BRITISH OVERSEAS AIRWAYS CORPORATION IN ASSOCIATION WITH QANTAS EMPIRE AIRWAYS LIMITED · SOUTH AFRICAN AIRWAYS · TASMAN EMPIRE AIRWAYS LIMITED

BEA

BRITISH EUROPEAN AIRWAYS

Artist unknown

1957

One of the most enlightened moves in
post-war British aviation was the establishment,
in 1946, of British European Airways with
responsibility for domestic and short-haul European
routes. Its motto was *Clavis Europae*, the Key
to Europe, and by the end of the Fifties it flew
more than half of all scheduled air traffic on the
routes it served. In 1974 it was dissolved, along
with BOAC, to form British Airways

BEA

BRITISH EUROPEAN AIRWAYS

NORTH AMERICA
FLY THERE BY BOAC

Artist: **Hayes**

1953

Another strong portrait by Hayes, the creator
of the stunning Australian bathing beauty on
Page 109. This time the subject is a rugged American
cowboy, cigarette in hand, but quite nattily
dressed; the detail on the saddle is particularly fine,
as is the texture of the Indian blanket. Since Britain
was granted landing rights only at cities on the
eastern seaboard of the United States, BOAC
passengers wishing to travel to the Wild West
were forced to transfer to an American
airline in New York or Washington

SOUTH AMERICA
FLY THERE BY BOAC

Artist unknown

1959

A riot of colour and excitement
characterises this 1959 poster for BOAC's
South American service, restored in 1958 after a
four-year gap caused by a shortage of aircraft
following the Comet disaster. The beautiful dancer,
her earrings swaying as she does, sports a
Carmen Miranda head-dress which threatens to
become entangled in the mass of bright streamers.
Visible in the background are the lights of
Rio and the cut-out faces of happy revellers,
some with animal masks

South America
fly there by
B·O·A·C
BRITISH OVERSEAS AIRWAYS CORPORATION

USA

FLY BOAC

Artist: **Abram Games**

1959

A novel treatment of the cowboy
theme by Abram Games, who handles it with his
usual wit and surreal touch, as the ten-gallon hat
turns into a skyscraper and vice versa.
Unlike much of Games's other work which shows a
subtle blending of hues (See Pages 57 and 93),
here the colours are limited to blue, white, and
two shades of fiesta red. The deliberately rough cut
outlines belie Games's elegant draughtsmanship,
while the familiar Speedbird symbol takes
on an unaccustomed jaunty air

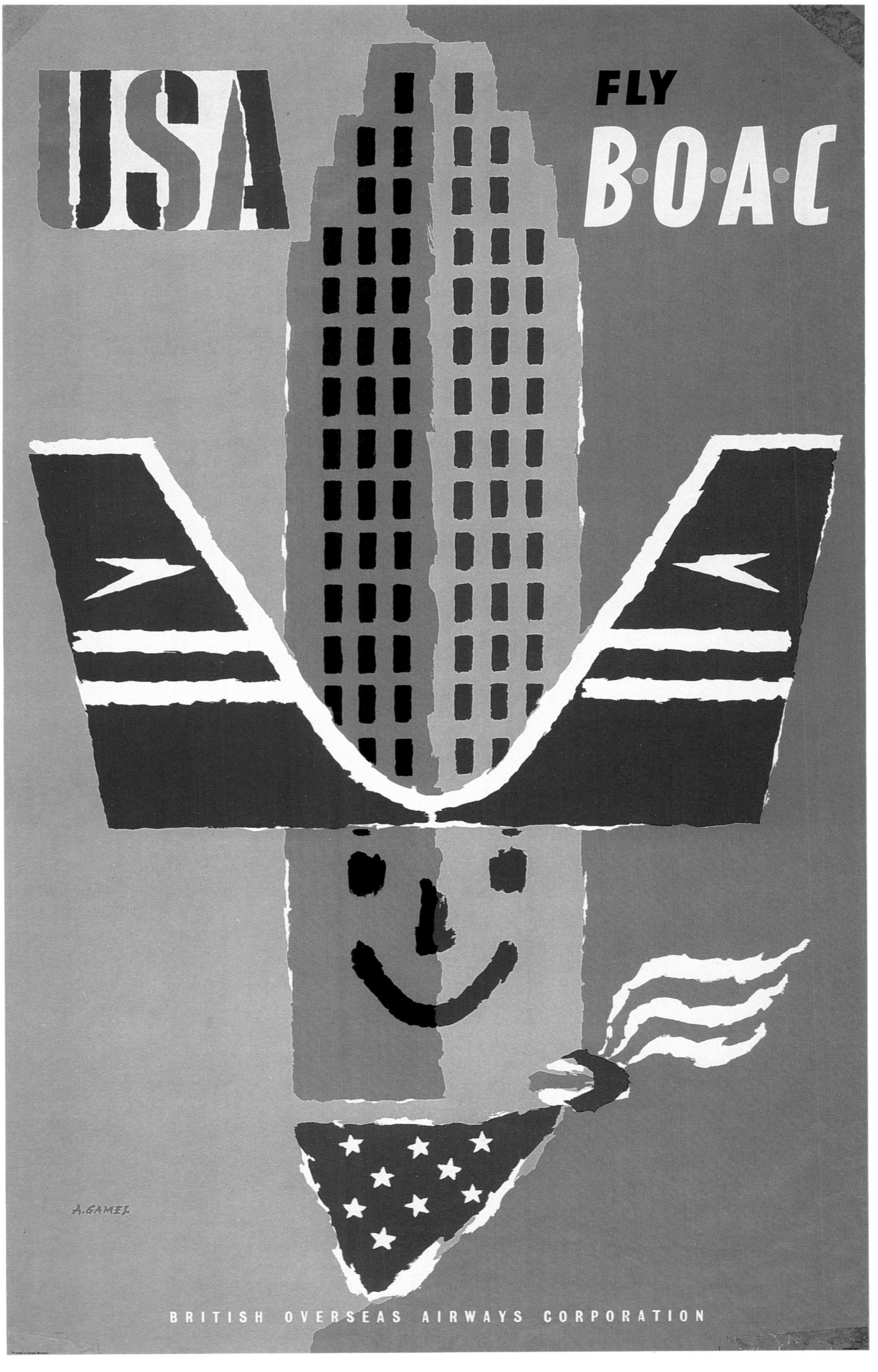
USA
FLY
B·O·A·C
A. GAMES
BRITISH OVERSEAS AIRWAYS CORPORATION

ON BUSINESS FLY BEA

British European Airways

Artist: **Abram Games**

1956

Here Abram Games turns his fertile
imagination to the British businessman, suggested
by the briefcase and rolled umbrella, propellers
sprouting from his pin-striped sleeve.
In 1956, the year of this poster,
BEA carried almost twice as many passengers
within Europe as Air France, its nearest rival.
The decision to create BEA as a separate airline
specifically for European and domestic traffic
had proved to be a wise one

ON BUSINESS FLY
BEA

BRITISH EUROPEAN AIRWAYS

INDEX OF ARTISTS